Differentiated Sameness

A Collection of Sufi Poems

SHAYKH FADHLALLA HAERI

Zahra Publications

Published by Zahra Publications
PO Box 50764
Wierda Park 0149
Centurion
South Africa

Email Info@sfhfoundation.com
www.sfhfoundation.com
www.zahrapublications.com

Designed and typeset by Quintessence Publishing
Cover Design by Quintessence Publishing

ISBN: 978-1-928329-18-3

Table of Contents

BETWEEN FINITE AND INFINITE

TIMELESS

About the Author

Born in Karbala, Iraq, Shaykh Fadhlalla Haeri, comes from severalgenerations of religious and spiritual leaders. After several years living and working in the west, he rediscovered the universal relevance of the Qur'an and Islamic teachings for our present day. His emphasis has been on transformative worship and refi nement of conduct, as preludes to the realisation of the prevalence of Divine Grace. He considers that the purpose of life is to know and resonate with the eternal essence of the one and only Lifegiver— Allah

Acknowledgements

The author would like to thank Ahmed Baasith Sheriff, Zaheer Adam, Hasnayn Ebrahim, Muneera Haeri, Muna Bilgrami and Leyya Kalla for their assistance in bringing this collection of poems to production.

Introduction

The human journey on earth is from low, basic sentiency towards the highest level of consciousness. From childhood on we are challenged to witness, experience, and choose what is better for our happiness. With awakening you discover that, in truth, there is no differentiation or separation as everything is still contained within absolute, unitive reality.

Oneness is the only truth and the process of differentiating between what is good and what is not is like coming across milestones along that path. We differentiate in order to be content with the connectedness that leads to essential original Oneness.

Human consciousness links the infinite unseen with finite sensory experiences. These poems are like flags. The material is a language or brush strokes indicating transitions between the boundless and the limited, within and beyond time and space, like flags on a temple reminding us of our transitory earthly journey and how magnificient it is if we are aware of its timeless grace.

Within Space-Time

Acceptance

The old man, quarrelsome
grumpy and depressed
family and friends avoiding him now
long suffering wife still caring
I'm used to it, she said
I do what I can
half a century of practice
she said with a reconciled smile
I could cope after giving up judgment
expectations or the idea of happiness and joy
sometime in the future
the old man's nastiness has helped me
no confusion of choice
just acceptance
then came trust and love
then truth showed everywhere
a wise voice had said
acceptance, repentance
and cosmic resonance.

Nationhood

We were not allowed to be a nation
we screamed
we killed
we escaped
and we wept
we even forgot what it was all about.
We were then allowed to vote
acquire a new tribal identity
and care for personal gains
wealth, status and power
pursue illusions of independence
personal and national
like everyone else
globally confused
but this time
with a flag
and serious financial debts.

Forbidden Land

Incomplete development
where will it end?
pain accompanies
growth
limited and conditioned
with an end in sight
with the next beginning
Where is the shore of the promised land?
When do we get there?
Don't tell me after the next war?
But I don't want to die
Are we all doomed?
Have we fallen into the forbidden land?

Pain

Wherever she turned
there were doubts and uncertainty:
what does the future hold?
It's all about that
isn't it?
A good fortune –
but no one can tell me
what that really is!
The sage says 'timelessness'
the philosopher says 'the real' –
but I still remain
in the pain
of ignorance
and the darkness of fear and sorrow.

New Home

She was desperate for a new home
a better cave
a happier womb
motherly phase over
children grown and gone
a new house needed
new friends filled with goodness and light
friends who travel lightly on the earth
lugging little physical or mental baggage
heavenly people on an earthly transit
like her
But where are they?
Will they take me as they find me?
Will they accept me?
Will I recognise them?
Oh God, I need to know!

Unlike Mother

Don't judge me by my mother
I am not like her
nor my sister
nor brothers
please excuse their crudeness
grossness
rudeness
I am not like them
I can't deny similarities
especially skin colour and
behaviour and culture
but don't judge me by my family
I am not like them
nor am I like me
that changes all the time
that is why
I don't know
who am I.

You Only Live Once

The President For Life
confessing to the priest
in between sobs
I have little time
I have no time
life is short and
mine is shorter
so much I can do now
so much I need to do
but life is short and I don't trust anyone
except me
well, maybe Jesus
but you understand me well, Father
or at least you are quiet and calm
I need to talk
I am really afraid of death
but no one can deny the mantra:
you only live once.

The Lesson of Serena Owletta

Absent for two weeks
she is back this morning.
Ten days of stillness
sitting on an egg – phantom or real?
Why is she back now, I asked her?
Silent and still, she tests me
her swivelling head lifts gracefully
then bows down in contentment and wisdom.
She looks at me, her big eyes saying
I just did what was to be done
obeying the moment.
It is you humans who seem confused and unreliable
restlessly obsessed
with power and knowledge
not present
distracted from the perfection of beingness.
The eternal moment is ever present.
I follow and obey
I sit, I fly
I return, I sit again
Perfection is in the flow and I know only that.
Then two eggs hatched and
two beautiful chicks emerged.

Within a few weeks they began to fly.
A few months on
parents and offspring often perch
together on the oak –
best time to hear them hoot
soon after sunset.

Noisy Silence

I kept quiet
still and almost absent
those around weren't happy with my power of silence
I was content and ignored the chatter
silent and noisy
the usual human conflict
living whilst dying
not as a resolving challenge
biographies built on heaps of decomposing rubbish and
trash masked with hesitant smiles
that is how we polluted the earth with our inner mess
then express shock at the outer disaster
environmental degradation
blaming it on others
As for the people nearby
who only hope to hear what confirms their views
seeking news and views
to ensure survival and palliative contentment
everyone wants to hear what confirms their mind's clutter
Oh God, I need your help
I said to myself
but this time aloud
then returned to silence.

Silent Conversation

Silence whispered in my ear
"to know the story of earth
ask the heavens"
Then it whispered in the other ear
"as for the story of heavens, ask the earth" –
identical twins separated in space

But to know who you are there is no one to ask
just embrace silence and pray for grace
the rest are colourful traps in time and space
guarded by fears, desires,
distractions and other fantasies,
preparations for suffering
sometimes veiled by values
like kindness, freedom
or service to others
and countless others mirages
in life's vast desert.

Only through acceptance
are such snares transcended
and by grace you may realise
the ever-present essence
from where silence and sound emerge:
your own soul,
the origin of all conversations.

Not Abandoned

I am not forgotten
they called today
wanting to see me
I am missed they said
but in truth they don't know who
they are
we all live in confused amnesia most of the time
on rare occasions we are called normal
I did have the illusion of missing something or other
or fearing abandonment
then I switched to actually desiring seclusion
they think I found something
special and most valuable
they are both right and wrong
everyone seeks his treasure
looking for it ensures its elusiveness
masses of earthly collusions
with no clear conclusions
unless you abandon whatever is on earth
everything within space and time
conditioned
limited
and ever changing.

Unforgettable Truth

You forgot again
naturally
you are often absent minded.

Awareness of the moment
is the start of the path of true remembrance
pure and complete awareness
unattached to anything
neither time nor place
a pure imprint of the eternal
perfect presence.

Most people are like you
living in darkness and confusion
but for your own sake
remember
before it's too late
be present at the moment
when creation began
at that point everything
is present
even our moment in time
now.

Cosmic Invention

Once anything exists
it tends to continue
in form or meaning
so who are you complaining to?
you got into it
you allowed it to touch you
how can anyone help?
at best you meet a mirror
whilst habits continue
celebrating eternal life
As for personal life
it is stuck between fear and hope
so forget it
or return it
to the Cosmic Inventor.

Special or Not?

The sage said
I am only one
of millions the same
only slightly different
yet you think you are special
as do most others
Now reflect upon who you are?
And who are they?
Where are you all from?
And where are you going to?
Sameness exists due to difference
Everyone is ordinary as a human
and special always
because of life
now enjoy the two as one.

Endless Need of Time

I need more time
don't ask how long
I don't know what is enough
all I know is that time is short
the cause of my insecurity
fear of loss
and all that is unknown
and that is a lot
for all of that
for God's sake
give me more time
that is why I desire
the timeless.

Constant Needs

I need you
please tell me you know
tell me you trust me
I need reassurance
less bereftness
but who am I
unreliable
at all times
I know that much
that little
please help me
I need to reconcile
past, present and future
I need continuity
I need dependability
I need honesty
please help me
now.

Joyful Sacrifice

At first
a few leaves were shed
then small twigs
and all the elderly branches
then the whole tree
falling with thunderous majesty
the roots lifted above nearby shrubs
celebrating loyalty to the cycle of life
by declaring the end
of separation from origin
the end of a temporary phase
of appearing
above and below ground
declaring presence
and the drive for fulfilment
celebrating the truth of timeless Oneness.

The Remedy of Absence

Better to sleep
shut down the senses
sights, insights and awareness
absent from pleasure and pain
embracing the void
the origin of all absence and presence
and time and other distractions
for a while or longer
Then repeat this experience
all life long for
real presence and its favour
may then touch you.
After years of drought and darkness
the thorn bush noticed its thirst
the desert didn't care
nor did the oceans or clouds
nor the star crudely labelled
with long numbers and letters
A new challenge
maybe a new discovery
bearing my name – a futile tag
descriptions and definitions

continue in absurdity
fitting circles within triangles
and claiming efficient outcomes
a civilisation of absurdities
fleeting within misty space and time
claiming exactitude
hoping for deliverance
through precision and exact failures
impetuous denials hiding all needs and attachments
hiding human frailty
hiding the light
that illumines all realities
always transient and yet constant.

Selectivity

Our senses are selective
limited and proximate
you close your ears at loud sounds
you protect your eyes from the glare
you avoid pain and whatever else
disconnects or smells of death
we are obsessed
with life
and the continuity of its grace
including fear and sorrow
or darkness and confusion
to avoid
remaining ever-alive
as the light of life
within my heart
and yours
and all life
Ever-glorious.

Best Choice

In truth
all choices and desires
end up as one choice
the best
the most appropriate
the perfect match
the right link
in the chain of time
just that.

Love and Lies

You lied to me
in the old village
we both lied even more
until we met again
in the big city
greater lies
civilized and polite
desperate for life and light
it is love that carries us through
it is love that is the source of all
it is also love that is the destiny of all
our lies are the dark shadow of this truth
in truth there is only
Truth.

Candle Light

I lit my candle
for the day
then lit another
for yesterday
and other days
where darkness prevailed
every day into the night
a lonely candle fluttered
and shared some light
brought to remind the living ones
that light produces shadows
and illusions
Light is the origin
and destiny
all shadows are reminders
of suffering and distractions
As for now
light more candles
until all that remains are
flickering lights that dance
like human souls
illumined and illuminating
surrounded by shadows.

No More Now

The real problem is
now
and that is where the solution is
in the Now
If it were not for that
there would be neither here nor there
nor anywhere else
nor any other time
beginnings cannot appear
all ends disappear
no problems or solutions
that is where people die
without a cause or excuse
to live for a while
and worry about death
here and now were ever-united
giving rise to illusions
needing now and later
endless conclusions.

Ice Desert

We were warned
about hungry wolves
roaming the harsh frozen land
popular now with extreme adventurers
every year people were attacked
dozens of adventurers bitten in one leg
every man wrote a book
about losing a leg in the wolf attack
strong tents and sealed sleeping bags were not enough
one guide specialized in recounting gruesome tales
and the wolves' preference for snatching legs
humans continue to face death
bemoaning the ice desert with its roaming packs
of desperate wolves
under the pretense of enjoying extreme exposure
sampling the boundaries and limits of earthly living
invertedly desiring comfort and ease
never content
in any time or
any place.

Can Your See?

Did you hear the baby cry?
Did you see the sun set and rise again
or was it us falling down?
What goes up, they say
will always come down, they say
among other wise noises
What comes always goes, they say
but no one asks to where?
Or why?
Or from where?
By whose orders or will, would I ever know?
Would you ever know or know how to have a happy ending?
Or is it a fairy tale in black and white
with a touch of grey in the middle?
Life descending and then ascending
if only we could see.

Pseudo Confidence

Truth
sneaks
in
without permission
or expectations
like a flash of light
illuminates and dazzles
and then vanishes again
leaving us bewildered and confused
only for a moment
when we return
confused now by normality
for everyone agrees
it is like this
all the time
history proves that
so does scripture
that God said
this is meant to be
true forever
meanwhile
everyone remains confused
pretending to be confident.

Traitors

The traitors were killed
seven people including two defectors
a reporter
confessing himself as a serious offender
not believing in anything or taking sides
a most dangerous being
accepting and rejecting at the same time
a traitor of elaborates human values
fake rules and laws
temporary and ever-changing
yesterday's criminal is today's hero
one day in jail
next year a sinking face on national currency
now try to catch
the real human traitor.

Time Beyond

Time has come
honored by affliction
no refuge
no respite
only patience
death-perfecting stillness
nearest to source
absolute
constant
the origin of every instant
only known to those
who live in time
and beyond.

Escaping Loneliness

Noise and distraction
temporarily filled up
loneliness
physical and emotional
the heart's loneliness
is from life itself
from Truth
from the essence of Source
none other than the light in your heart
resonate within you
its language is beyond dualities
of good and bad
or space and time
or human comprehension
beyond all emotions and attentions
illusions or conclusions.

Perpetuated Loneliness

Try again, stupid! Wisdom said
Don't be lonely, find a partner!
All creatures go in pairs
but so does human misery
Countless illusions pair up in
distracting absurdities
anything to avoid the ever-present Truth
Oneness traps you
through fear, sorrow and suffering
avoiding Oneness
bestows loneliness
with new regrets and blames
apparent connections with toxic temporary relief
followed by pain
and loneliness again.

Traps of Loneliness

It is human nature to fear loneliness
to fear the darkness of the ego-self
driven to get out of that trap
not by adding another burden
another confused lonely being
bringing a different version of the human tragedy
leading to the tragi-comedy of
separation and duality
confirmed by other feeble minds
hiding in a global cave
labelled 'human reality' and 'normality'
deaf to the true voice of truth
and blind to the sacred light of dualities and loneliness
unity hidden behind the true origin of all
and its destiny
perfect Oneness.

Towards Perfection

None of us are perfect
no one is ever perfect
so conventional wisdom goes
but half-way only
As for the other half of wisdom
seek the perfect always!
Why?
When you know everything is in flux and changing
it's surely absurd
to seek a situation
that is constant and perfect
unless it is a light
that draws us
to a higher state of perfection
where our soul or spirit's origin resides
with the Eternal
utterly
Perfect.

No Choice

You have no choice
but to desire the best always
no choice in avoiding sorrow or grief
and fearing loss and death
no choice in loving
your own soul's beauty and perfection
watching the ego
a shadow that lurks
a shadow due to the light
of the soul or spirit
no choice in accepting the trap
of human limitations
yearning for the boundless
no choice in desiring
the freedom to choose
the most appropriate
and the best.

Living Trace

He asked if I remembered him
an old friend
to be honest or just kind
not remembering much of the past
being polite
playing it safe
avoiding emotions
delusions woven in time
a jumble of past confusions
extracted for a moment
a museum piece
brought to life
by a living gaze
a beam of life
bringing alive
a forgotten trace.

A Most Crucial Issue

It used to be
the Meaning and Purpose of Life
with addenda
such as the Nature of God
and the Life of the Hereafter
and How to Reach Paradise
and other metaphysical, theological
and philosophical issues
but my friend was direct and personal
"How can I always be happy?"
he asked with total self confidence
I too was direct and brief
cutting past fear, sorrow, disappointment
and any distraction from being
fully present
in the immensity
of the now
In one long breath I said
it's easy if you are determined
serious and follow a plan
that takes you out of the illusion
of your usual identity
In his silence I hear

serious contemplation
Trust and flow I concluded
you need a few friends and maybe teachers
prayers for grace and guidance
from within your own heart
He needs to trust and flow
I thought to myself as I walked away.

Smiling Face

I do fear loss and loneliness
I do fear bad endings
I fear old age and dementia
I fear mental illness
I have seen it and was horrified
I need reassurance but no one gives it to me
religious healers and prayers have failed
yet I still look for assurance
Whoever tried to help lacks credibility
no one is exempt
no one is excluded
no one is uncertainty
everyone is caught within the divine web
it's born within us
to remind us of our vulnerability
human frailty and weakness
yet we admire and desire
strength and power
is that pushing against the natural order?
Why this futile fight?
Is it to give up all and to be at one with the light?
The face of cosmos says yes
with a smile.

Spare His Life

Kill me instead
cried the mother
whose young son
was caught stealing
by the legal gangsters
Please spare him
her eyes weeping
her voice screaming
her arms pointing towards heaven
His life is just beginning
I have lived it all
the good and the bad
and the very bad
The young officer said
we can't arrest you for his protest
we are a democracy now
you would have been killed a decade ago
under our despotic supreme leader
but now we have a new law
we have freedom of speech
and a bit for judicious journalism
so you can weep and scream

but we are taking your son
But please take me instead
the mother cried
and the young officer responded
We can only go by physical identity
if you can become him we will do that
as humans we are still clumsy creatures
electrons are ahead
they behave as a particle or as wave
we are not there yet.

The Truth in Me

I make so many mistakes
and try to hide many of them
although I know the truth will shine
hopefully one day
there will be no more mistakes
The sage said that will come after death
not before
You need to be humbled by mistakes
so celebrate your errors
and celebrate the perfect day
celebrate our desire for perpetual perfection
celebrate truth
celebrate its timelessness
celebrate your journey
grappling with it, to it, unto it
just celebrate.

Between Finite and Infinite

Eternal Truth

Some other time
in another place
truth may shine
its light
with no shadows
no fear
no ignorance
no otherness
no absence
only Presence
perpetually divine.

The Way Out

Don't block my view
I want to know what is there
further along
Where will this quest end?
fear and hope are my two legs
driven by the desire to know
the drive for freedom
from everything
including the idea of freedom
moving towards the new horizon
the abode of no-where-ness
but for now, please let me see
feel, smell and hear
what is here and there
my mind demands
What I really need is the way out of here
to what is out there and everywhere
without denying what is here
please help me.

Togetherness

Where did you go?
When did you go?
And why?
I feel lonely and abandoned
lost even to myself
to time and place
even the spider's web had vanished
so did the voice of complaint or blame
all seems lost
I feel bewildered
then the voice catches me,
Where were you?
otherness is here
only to reflect Oneness
the only path to heavens
reaches a gate of two sections
they open and shut together
casting a shadow of oneness
the mother
the father
of togetherness.

Now and Forever

Now you want to share and care
connecting and relating
climbing the ladder of consciousness
leaving yesterday's care
to live fully in the moment
without fear or sorrow
only a trace of yesterday
and a few other lost days
remain
to share with a few or more
as and when
then you plead for time and stop
and a voice cries
it never began!
never ever
then you pray
for eternal presence
now and forever.
Oh God, I need you
now
before now
and after forever.

Lost and Found

How can I know you
or know Rumi
or anyone else
when I don't know myself?
Whatever appears will change
before I can even describe it
unacceptable
as all lies are
unreliable
sparks caught in darkness
appearing as monuments
anything can happen
anytime and any place
suffering, fears and pains
natural outcomes
like other distractions
of fancy attractions
as it is found truth is lost
unless
your mind is still
your heart is present
and your inner light
shines now and forever.

Losing Identity

It is here and now
It is here and everywhere always
life's grace enables
sight, sound and movement
darkness' real identity is light
failure's real remedy is knowledge
stepping aside from all success and failure
the perfect present awaits you
where loneliness lost its dark shadow
due to unconditional love
suffering and grief are held back at the gate
of the city of joy
where countless universes
from the one cosmic origin
express all
ever there, here and everywhere
So where are you
And who are you
And where is it not?
It is all these
to be witnessed
then all earthly illusions
are lost.

Triumph of Life

As they had come
so will they go
As they had won
so will they lose
Whatever is born will surely die

When life touched you
it obsessed you
and possessed you
forever

Truth is at one with life
and life protects life
but within our earthly womb
through darkness we perceive a light
to know anything, we start with awareness
caught in the web of
space and time
to learn about home
we follow the transitory one
leading to the eternal origin of life
pure life
pure triumph.

The True Journey

Go where there is no sound
no space
no movement
no time
Go to where it all began
and where all ends
Go to where there is no beginning or end
to the country that has no map or visas or a language
to where no questions are asked
where everyone is at One
and no one discusses freedom
or liberation
Go to where there is no lost or found
Go to where you experience that everything is there
without occupying space
where you cannot describe anything
Go where you cannot go any further or nearer
Go without going
on this true journey.

In Perpetuity

It was a big watermelon
many of us enjoyed it
distracted folk enjoying the taste and aroma
through lips
and countless taste buds
the silent watermelon surrendered
with grace
passing its message through its seeds
small black seeds telling the whole story
an excuse to connect and continue
to glorify life
as it knows itself
like every other story in history or before
please let us read it
then we can dance to its music
while nature's chorus connects meanings and forms
here, there and everywhere
at all times and before time
in perpetuity.

Going Places

We are driven
to explore, discover and act
'getting on,' we say
'progressing,' we say
'evolving and developing,' others may say
'towards higher consciousness,' some may say
'towards truth' yet others may say
words and sounds attempt to explain
placate and connect to reason
like the stars and all that exists
everything moves on toward origin
Where do you begin?
Are you happy when it ends?
Where are you going?
How long will we play act?
In truth, there is no leaving, reaching, or return
a bubble on the ocean bounces with the waves
part of the ocean
totally connected
but what about the ocean itself?
Only by grace we think, hope and imagine
we are going somewhere

we are useful, successful
or even important
It is also only by grace
that we take its Light
for granted.

Truth of Lies

You are leaving again
you've been lying all along
I know
I've done the same
passion for life and its truth
beyond mind and other comical
tragedies such as the absurdity of birth
ending in death
Where is hope?
And lasting celebration?
all postponed for our animal survival
the joy of emergence to light
and perpetual life
the river of hope leads to the original spring
where pure consciousness prevails
enveloping every beginning and every end
that is the truth
hidden within every lie
what we call normal human life
and when the inner soul
leaves its earthly trap
there remains only truth
with no shadows or lies.

Alone

You left me too soon
a clear mirror
revealing all now
the perfect Presence
no confusion
no loneliness
eternal soul
that is the party
not to be missed.

Friendly Counsel

The two of you need to be reconciled
the human side
with its changing identities
and the spirit or soul
without clear definition or mental comprehension
no option except balancing
human and the divine
seamlessly connected
wisdom, rationality, personality
drives to be fulfilled
emerge due to power of your soul
humanity and its limitations emanate and return
to eternal source
intellect and reason also point to this truth
and desire it
and the light of the heart reaffirms it –
your spirit knows itself
if only you can listen to it
you have the best of friends
your light and shadow
friends
mate and soul mate
at One.

Perpetual Abode

Goodness seems short-live
its fountain of origin
is ever-living
We yearn for that true goodness
we are obsessed with eternal goodness
obsessed with the ever-perfect
ever present
a state without an abode
where real home is
on earth and elsewhere
all being prepared
for perfect goodness
in perpetuity.

Rejoice

Rejoice
rejoice again
in truth, you have no choice
celebrating origin
past, present and future and ever
celebrating life
life's glory
self-declaring
blissfully radiating
through all that exists
according to its potential to express its original joy
your purpose and duty reflect the joyful harmony
dazzled
by the light of One
reflecting beams and colours of the One and only One
otherwise darkness prevails
disconnecting all goodness and hope
As for you, do your best
through goodwill
good intention
good actions beyond the lower self
then express gratitude

sing and dance to the harmony
of the majesty
and beauty
of the One.

Love

Love will guide you
always, every time, in every place
unconditional love – gate to unity
no fear or sorrow
love honours your soul
self lost for a minute
as light of soul shines
love from the higher you
affecting lower states
cleansing your heart
then echoes the truth – lights and delights
Love leads to forever
no self left
love has taken you
to the real you
the light of life
within you
without it you are a walking corpse
with pure love
you are taken
to   pure inner
light.

Not Enough

Once experienced, it is not enough
once I see, feel and touch it
it's never enough
you know it is not good enough
nothing is ever enough in quality or quantity
whatever is defined or bound is not enough
we call it boring or unimportant
ignorable
like most relationships
Only when there is no 'me'
separate or independent
with an elusive identity
only then
is there hope
of glimpsing completeness
beyond pain, pleasure or need
where 'enough' and contentment
perfection
beyond measure
beyond pleasure
delighting with what is not enough
and beyond enough
perfect Presence.

Very Special

You are one of millions
the same as the rest
yet different
You think you are special
as do most others
But then who are you?
And who are they?
Who is ordinary?
And who is special?
You are both ordinary and extra-ordinary
same as the other millions
slightly different in flavour
all alive due to miraculous life
born to die and discover
eternal life
Your cosmic soul
ever there
most, most special
beyond anything the mind considers
a miracle.

Perpetual Light of Light

Being alive
A prelude to
obsession with life
boundless without beginnings or end
when life touches you and I
we are instantly obsessed
with its timeless boundlessness
our short earthly identity with fear and suffering
veiling the eternal reality of life
experienced through the lenses of duality
searching for unity of cosmic Light
and its eternal Reality
its cosmic nature
its beauty and majesty
driven by grace of
light of Life.

Forgetfulness

What a gift
to forget
also
thank God for remembering
boundaries and limitations
Forgetfulness is original
there was nothing to remember
then countless entities emerged
in heaven and on earth
all in transit
Forgetfulness is due to rememberance
death obliterates all
body, mind and ego vanish
into the ocean of unseen truth
with grace of hope and trust
Forgetfulness renews hope
to accept and cope
day after day, year after year
self-delusion
self-deception "it wasn't so bad after all" –
or was it worse?
I forgot.

Pleasantries

Please tell me
if I am friendly, cheerful and reliable
I like polite compliments
especially if there is truth in it
as life is full of noise
in the head, mouth and everything else

Lower nature often prevails
whilst higher nature is ever there
we are distracted, avoiding real issues
fearing death and departure
it is arrival to boundlessness
relief from uncertainties of dualities
awakening to the real
constant
with perpetual grace
perfect
no need for any
pleasantries.

One Story

Now please tell me the story
the real one not fiction
or figment of imagination
Who was it really?
What happened?
Why and how?
Please give me the real story
not the usual fake one
I only want the real truth
ever perfect
give me the real story
I want the story that reveals all
not just a bit of this now and a bit of then
I want the story before creation and continues ever after
this story never ends
with death or new religions
the story worth hearing is ever present
worth telling
worth living
that is the real story
thank you God
for this promise
fulfilling all hopes and desires.

To the One

Stop disturbing
I need peace
silence and stillness
I need to stop

I need everything and nothing
I need to see it all
with insight
I need to know it all
then I need to be at one
with it all

Please show me the way
to the one
who is everywhere
not confined
every time from before time
please
O generous One.

Light of the Heart

When will peace prevail?
when will problems end?
when will I be content?
when will the world live in harmony?
when will I know my own nature?
when will I know the nature of existence?
when will I know the nature of nature?
and what is before and after?
what is the nature of time and space?
when will I know the nature of light?
when will I be at one
with the light in my heart?

Divine Expressions

Everything
in
existence
tells
its
story
as
messages
reflecting the origin
of all
and destiny
of all
grace
to
grace.

Truth

Most perplexing
losing myself first
then losing all else
whenever I am absent
it is effulgent
whenever it appears I am lost
there to be seen
the true
divine dance.

Differentiated Sameness

It is always the same
and yet different –
differentiated sameness!
back to the start!
you begin and end!
slow or fast –
back to the start!
always experiencing now
its echoes
past or future
here and there
everything changes
ever different
but I am the same –
so it seems to me!
I think.

Disguised Sameness

You may do
much or less
or undo
or redo
traces appear
only to disappear
or change
emerging from a light
named constancy
coloured like rainbows
then subsiding back
to Oneness
the home of immensity
and where
everywhere you look
it is the utterly the same
with a new name
why where and how?
after endless discovery
you awakened to disguised sameness
original Oneness.

Celebration

Do what you like or dislike
at the end as at the beginning
timeless boundlessness
ever the same
veiled from the doer
who sings a little
weeps a little
then with confusion
old age and other delusions
returns to origin
perfect destiny
worthy of celebration
in perpetuity.

Knowledge Knows

I never knew who I was
until you said you know
only now I know no one knows
but light knows itself
so does knowledge.

An Ordinary Special

One day
I will be discovered
they will know
how special I am
rare, unique and most precious
those who ignored and disliked me
without guilt or sorrow
and those who loved and cherished me
pleasurable connection
admitting my ordinariness
I love the special in me
and now nothing matters but
to enjoy the new me
forever and ever
in time and eternally
locally and universally.

Accept and Flow

No others
not even you
have any say or control
other than to accept and flow
as all that appears
mere shadows
moving in space and time
only to disappear
whatever emanates will surely return
declaring with passion and honesty
there is only that
that is what it is
It is
truly is.

Speed

Get there now
even faster if you can
before now
then pursue a new project
faster
even before the project began
then desire more and even more
but whatever you do
don't ever blame time!
or deny
human inadequacy
and insanity
appearing as anxiety
fears, sorrows and
other sufferings
labelled and ranked
as mental imbalances
or psychosis
appearing with speed
since we haven't learned
to stop.

Facts or Fictions

We need myths and legends
to connect the most unknown
with transient reality
within time

Without legends, ideas and fantasy
we feel disconnected
and what we call normal
is most insufficient
a semblance of security
or trust and steadiness

We need the ancient tales
so that our transit on earth
gains a higher reference
and is acceptable for a while
in place and time
as we return
to timelessness
without fiction
or mental addiction.

Self-Declaring

Whatever you do
or don't
self-declares
life's rainbows
whatever appears
or exists
a message in perpetuity
self to self
a full circle
a full life
life from life
self declaring.

Wait

Wait
more time is needed
always
never enough
as long you experience time
it's never enough
but wait
complain more if that helps
What else is patience
other than objecting to time
where disease and cure
are hand in hand?
But as for now
just wait
time is not ready for you
your birth was before time
so just wait.

Magic and Light

More mountains appeared
as the mist lifted
in blue and violet
now after now
fainter and further
and when the sunlight became stronger
all merged with light
losing identity
and submerged into apparent reality
there is always more in the universe
than we think or imagine
yet all vanish when light submerges their mind
light produces discernment
light blurs boundaries and separation
all tricks begin with light
and all tricks end with light
and every snapshot is framed
by darkness cast by light
all miracles due to light
magical light.

Presence

They have all gone
some may never come back
a few may appear again
such is our world
arrivals and departures
until the final exit
closing all chapters
end of all uncertainties
a glimmer of reality
passing shadows and shapes
mostly bitter-sweet
with touches of truth
if you can sense it
if you connect with it
if you seek it and want it
that aroma tells you
of the abode of perfect Presence.

Where were You?

Where were you when I called
when I cried
when I died?
Where were you before I arrived on earth
without me?
What awaits me?
the uncertainty of it all
promising the good
flashes of delight
in foggy light
here and there, occasionally
But where were you when I died
when I laughed and cried
when I waved and called
before I flew back
before I arrived?
Where were you?
Where were you before I lost me?

Tuesday

They told me it is Tuesday
a different day
ignoring the sameness
of everyday
"yesterday's gone," they said
To where? Why? And how?
garments of minds and other fictions
a bundle of connecting mirrors
giving the illusion of movement
change and speed
giving rise to desires and fears
hoping to connect all
and be at one with all
but then all days vanish
and space and time return
to eternity
no you and I anymore
with Tuesday gone falsehood is gone
truth remains ever the same.

Lasting Contentment

You will never be truly content
How can you ever stop at limits?
How can little be enough?
You are driven to beyond bounds
where home was before being earthbound
And the drive to be content
relentless and futile
How to accept limitations
whilst questing boundlessness?
Suspended between changes and stillness
and the elusive pursuit of confused humans
with a divine soul ever-perfect
whilst giving rise
to all shades of darkness and distractions
all illumined
by the One
and Only One.

The Perfect Partner

The quest for a soul mate
the incessant drive
for the perfect partner and companion
an uncertain outcome at best
more often a breakdown
accompanied by blames and claims
everyone is wrong except oneself!
Where does it end?
Where did it even begin?
What a divine plot
which is only revealed
by the quest for origin and the thirst for Oneness
light of the soul
when all shadows are lost
where original light dispels
illusions of otherness
what is left is
the cosmic song of Oneness
the soul's true mate!

Eternal

The patient is dead now
lost to patience
due to impatience
lost to time
and place
in union
with unity
truth
reality
oneness
boundless
timeless
the real reward
constant
absolute
One
eternally.

Time of Life

Is time your enemy or friend?
Who is your best friend?
Who is your worst enemy?
Does it really matter?
You are surrounded by enemies and friends
sometimes you don't know who they are!
that is because you don't know what time is
you may know what time of day it is
but what about the time of life?
nothing disturbing
nothing challenging
no out and no in
no high or low
where all is still
in its eternal
cosmic harmony
in life.

All in Time

Is this the best or worst time in your life?
What about other best and worst times?
What about short or long times?
Then what about no time?
Or all the time?
You are obsessed with life in time
and beyond
reconciling this moment with eternity
trying to step out of the box of beginnings and ends
to touch the sacred heart
of eternal Presence
where change and time
are utterly silent
until creation begins
and you ask
why?
Every time.

Truth

Concern may rule the day
but where was it yesterday?
Where will it be tomorrow?
Humbled and harmonized at once
helpless and confused
to be released from
temporary illusions
years of sorrow
not later or tomorrow
now, in this instant
and forever
as truth resides
deep in every heart
effulgent as the sky
sometimes
and always
true.

One Question Only

"One question only,"
he begged
"Who are you?"
I was silent

To stop the mind's chatter
from that stillness
a voice pronounced
"a light with changing shadows
ever-changing realities
driven by the real
a confusion that discloses
its eternal fusion
the many from the one
they come at once
after which
no questions or answers
ever
not even One."

Light in Time

At that time
it seemed perfect
but not anymore
mockery of what is real
deceptions of illusions
at that time
and this time
at all times
confusing shadows
every place
every time
but once you see the light
there is only
Light
In its own
time.

The Hidden Gift of Loneliness

Due to grace
the soul shines upon the ego
transcending perpetual earthly loneliness
through meditation and silence
the eternal moment
takes you into the truth of eternity
now
from which all illusions of tragic absurdities
arise and subside
like the ocean's tide
and higher consciousness reveals
that all darkness and loneliness is due
to illusions of identity
separation from cosmic Oneness
and the trap of space and time
your loneliness was a life-line extended to you
to drive you
back to your own soul
and cosmic Oneness.

Lost and Found in Now

Greetings with hugs and embraces
soon subside
like an ocean wave
rising to a crest
only to fall
What was all that about?
Why does anything occur?
Why here and not there?
And who am I to know?
But before all of that
who am I really?
Where was I a thousand years ago?
and where in another thousand years?
But for now forget counting
be honest for a moment
less than a minute
only now
which continues forever.

To Know Truth

Now I cut my finger
labelled an accident
unfortunate incident
causing pain and care
agents of life
obsession with life
with or without blood
the flow of life is eternal
whereas events are tagged
as good or bad
reversing positions
as cheerful or sad
every awareness brings an end
and life has no beginning
nor does it end
my finger will never
know this truth or others
but
will I ever
know the Truth?

The Real Me

"Thanks for forgetting me"
I have never found the real 'me'
after much search and confusion
after years of hope and fear
after denials and lies
and upholding norms and reasons
with shades of dishonesty
age-old treasons and tricks

Then a wise one stopped it all
"Forget it all!"
after years of ascending consciousness
still occasionally as a dream or faint memory
a gentle voice smiles
with the absurdly insane question
"Who is the real me?"

Origins

We always love the big
sometimes also the small
we love speed, the instant
to be there, now, forever
there is more to life than success
but how much are needed?
only God knows, I remain ignorant
as I am in a perpetual quest
of the infinite and beyond time!
we talk of contentment
while contradictions, confusions and illusions
fill up my life
then comes the shock of the greatest unknown
revealing the original light
brighter than all lights
beyond all descriptions and definitions
giving rise to our temporary drives
to strive, attain and then again
move to where it all began
without end
divine origin.

One Light

To see
is to be confused
to misinterpret
to walk
is to deceive
movement, form and distance
to think
is to knock
on the house of life
seeking truth
another cover-up
a no-man's land
where anything can happen
real or false
with or without labels
where sight and insight
are at One.

Existential Loop

I forgot
I also remembered
that I forgot
again
what is consistent
again
is forgetting
and remembering
again and
again
consistently
an existential loop
in nature.

In Between

I look
I see and don't really see
I listen
I hear and don't really hear
I live
both alive and dead
I am
true and false
and the story continues
as it has always been
in time and beyond
with or without me
what majesty
beauty and perfection
with and without me
and my illusions and temporary condition
perfections of beingness
in between darkness
and light
hoping to be with
perpetual delight
and in between.

External Life

Please don't die before me
I can't live without you
your mirror perfectly reflects me
much of it unknown to me
that's why I can't live without you
you have shown the real me
without you there is only loss
I don't mind fog and darkness
but I treasure losing me to the real me
and the real me was seen through your mirror
human sanity
enhancing vanity
the human mirror reflects eternal life
and not the short lived ones we cling to
so don't die before me
or at least take me with you
I love eternal life.

Another Day

Another day after another night
Tuesday I think
surely to be followed
Wednesday I think
no beginning without ending and
no ending without beginning
scared of death
fear of ending
and unknown new beginning
circle that goes round
where a dot is the origin and end
of all circles, squares and other forms
It goes up or down and nowhere at all
surely this is THE holy puzzle
surely we are in it
surely it is within us
surely that is true
maybe I will know it
another day.

Timeless

Divine Lesson

Her hut was a hole
in the ancient city wall
a few meters away from the Indian ocean
the old lady smiled and cried at the same time
giving her the parcel of food
she pointed to the broken pot
with a toothless smile, hugging a cat
She said, "this morning, the cat jumped onto the shelf
and the only pot I had fell down and shattered"
she stroked the cat and smiled more
"I love the cat but I need food
I love life more
"the next world will be the same as you leave this"
the toothless mouth spoke
"I want to leave happy"
happy forever
that's what Krishna promised.

Pleasure of God

"To please God," the pious man announced confidently
"I serve for God's sake," he emphasized
a self-assured believer
humans desire goodness
and desire to spread it
without asking what is durably good?
the ultimate in cleverness and stupidity
appears in our actions
confused with our purposefulness
and desire to connect via usefulness
to alleviate obvious needs and suffering
for everyone hopes for a better tomorrow
but most also want it here and now
then what?
how long will contentment last?
is it always with God's pleasure?
where does that pleasure begin?
and where will it end?
As my desires never end
So I imagine God being the same.

Truth of Now

No way out
no way in
no out
no in
no sideways
no way
no space
no time
I now know all this
as I have lost everything else
as I am in the perpetual now
all lost
and all found
now.

To Know Truth

"Who are you to object?" he asked.
He then left us in suspense, with a ray of hope
before quenching our thirst
Whilst we were all lost
trusting our mistrust
waiting for the next breath
waiting for a better life
without knowing what it is or why
or for how long
where is the real story
and its end
without knowing its beginning
is it like truth, without a beginning
or an end?
only Truth knows truth.

Perpetual Love

Perpetual love has no mortality
no dignity
no knowledge
of what changes
except change itself?
Movement and change
announce the Ever-Constant
the Source of all dignity
honour and reality
of perfect love
in perpetuity.

Sacred Treasure

Everyone wants to tell a story
better than others
greater, bigger
never smaller
yet smaller than the smallest
is what truth tells us
revealing that the smallest beyond measure
is where the biggest beyond measure lies
one home
all other story tellers
declare some aspect
of the eternal story
within a measure
whoever has heard that story is transformed
bewildered by the sacred treasure.

One Author

It is all the same
except in name
there is a beginning
and there is an end
sometimes remembered
more often not
forgotten
energy and form appear
and then again not
some questions produce answers
except the whys or why nots
an exception may show
the illusion of the plot
and the author of time is
One Author.

The Mountain Friend

The distant mountain
one day clear and proud
another in mystical mist
today it embraced me
absorbed me
was me
before creation
or after its end
no me
no mountain
no distance
no time
no veils
only lights and shadows
connecting friends.

A Journey

The clapping thunder
flashing fear and hope
majesty and beauty
clear and obscure
hidden and visible
here but from there
one face with countless expressions
one instant
from timelessness
one light
countless shadows
and rainbows
punctuation marks
on the journey of earth
What a journey!

Source of Desires and Attachments

All due to love
desire for contentment
original loyalty and belonging
to perfect destiny
security and trust
radiating from unity
and primal love
all due to timeless
Oneness
source of all desires and attachments
emancipation and liberation
and all their shadows and darkness
of fears and concerns
entrapments and gloom
with delusions and illusions
distractions and destructions
emanating from the One
source of life
and existence
ever perfect
constant and perpetual.

Sacred Duality

The earthly womb of space and time
preparation by eternal grace
hidden to the eye
penetrating all existences
ever connected to their origin and souls
throbbing within every heart
responding to life
primal loyalty to original light
from where polarity and plurality emerged
sacred dualities confirming
the divine source
origin and destiny – unity
all expressing obsession and love
for the ever-present Oneness.

Discovering the Treasure

To see the magic of it all
from the most drab and ordinary
insight emerges from sight
revealing how special it is
the transitory reveals perpetuity
the origin always prevails
each speck of dust
reveals its universal origin
measureable size and durability
and other mental delusions
reducing the most precious jewel to a common pebble
loss of value
the ultimate loss
darkness of hell
but the heart promises paradise
heard from far and near
the divine call
revealing the treasure.

Songs of Time

Everyone is caught in my web
so declared Life
from there comes all the quests
webs within webs
many entangled
but each of them carries a trace of light
creating movement and action
creation and destruction
horrors and beauty
if you dance with the song
with the legs of beauty and majesty
you may touch timelessness
and the song that's forever.

Song of Space

I whispered to myself
piercing thunder
then space said
I can stretch
beyond limits and shrink below perception
I am everywhere and nowhere
in time and beyond time
my twin companion – time
is the conjurer of movement
I simply frame it
within boundaries
between heavens and earth
your midwife and your mother
born in the new land
all living creatures want more
of what they have
more time, more space
pushing the boundaries
all of it
within boundlessness.

Awe and More

I love a good surprise
willingly accepting
anything that touches the boundaries
of mind and its past
enjoying the awesome
higher zone of awareness
higher consciousness
timeless and infinite
most awe-inspiring
it may begin with love and reverence
a touch of glorious presence
not conceivable by a faint heart
concealed
slowly, even more slowly
revealed
awe after awe
until you're lost in awesomeness
on the shore of the Ever-Real.

Hopefulness

The door of hopefulness
leading to life's fullness
everything is alive
witnessing its perfect journey
towards the original illumination
ever-present
embraced by gratefulness
perfection
revealing itself
to the inner eye and insight
where time has stopped
and eternity ever present
expressed in every language
cosmic silence within every existence
stars, galaxies and other blips
expresses delights and hopefulness
sometimes shyly and quietly
sometimes a noisy celebration.

Perfect Time

Time is ever there
emerging from timelessness
ever-fresh and new
ever-generous
repeat opportunities
everytime
take it now
riding to eternity
from time to timelessness
that is loyalty
honesty
divine friendship.